ARES VS. ATHENA: WHO WON THE BATTLE?

MYTHOLOGY BOOKS FOR KIDS
CHILDREN'S GREEK & ROMAN BOOKS

In this book, we're going to
talk about the Greek god Ares
and the Greek goddess Athena.
So, let's get right to it!

Greek mythology was made up of teachings, legends, and myths. It was part of the religion in Ancient Greece. Their gods and goddesses had the same virtues and faults as human beings, except they were divine and much more powerful than humans.

STATUE OF ARES

THE HISTORY BEHIND ARES AND ATHENA

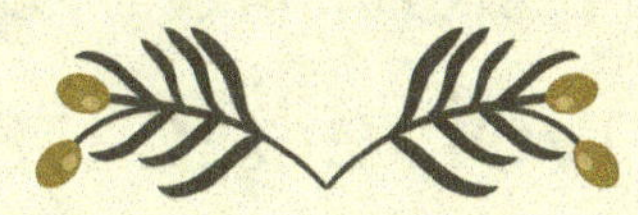

The Greek god Ares and his half sister, the goddess Athena, were rivals. In fact, the rivalry between this imaginary god and goddess was so powerful that it became part of the real world of Greek culture.

A res and Athena also represented different aspects of war. Ares was bloodthirsty. He seemed to enjoy war and killing. He often didn't seem to care which side he was on as long as he was involved in battle.

STATUE OF ATHENA

Athena was warlike as well, but she was also wise. She wanted to win the battle, but she wanted to do so with the least amount of killing. She was all about winning a war by using strategy not excessive brutality.

THE CITY-STATES OF SPARTA AND ATHENS

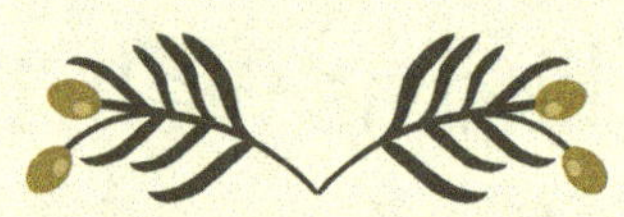

In the real world, the Greek city-states of Sparta and Athens were also enemies. They each aligned themselves with a different deity. The Spartans worshipped Ares as their god of war. Their values were based on power and military force. On the other hand, the Athenians worshipped Athena as the goddess of wisdom and war strategy.

SPARTAN SOLDIER

The citizens of each city-state hated each other and they were always battling. The problems between the rivals became so great that in 431 BC the Peloponnesian War broke out. This violent struggle between them lasted for twenty-seven years but for centuries afterwards the rivalry continued.

THE REASON THAT ARES AND ATHENA WERE RIVALS

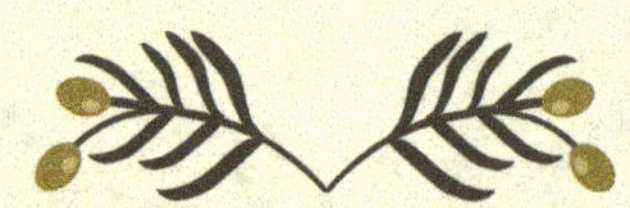

A res had a very hot temper and he was always eager to do battle. Athena was worshipped as the goddess of protection, security, and intelligent strategy. Those who worshipped Athena looked down on Ares because of his violent temper.

Because the Spartans worshipped Ares, the Athenians viewed the Spartans as hotheaded and ignorant just like the god they worshipped. On the other hand, the Spartans thought the Athenians were weak and they considered them to be cowards.

When Athena was born, she supposedly came directly from Zeus's skull. Zeus was the god of all the gods. Ares was immediately upset by his half-sister's presence. She threatened his position on Mount Olympus as god of war since she was also a goddess of war. The intelligent way in which Athena designed her wartime strategies threatened Ares' wartime success.

ZEUS

Eventually, Greek society got tired of this brutish, uncivilized god and they began to move away from worshipping him. In a sense, this was when Athena won one of the battles because she was still popular while Ares was phased out.

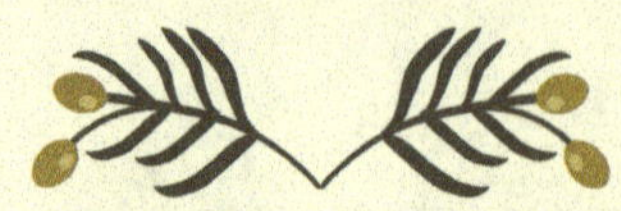

Both Homer as well as Euripides, who were famous Greek authors, wrote that these ancient ways of worship lasted through about 250 BC. Even though the worship of gods and goddesses began to disappear over time, the battles between the cults of Athena and her half-brother Ares continued.

STATUE OF ANCIENT GREEK POET EURIPIDES

WERE THERE SIMILARITIES BETWEEN ARES AND ATHENA?

Despite their differences, both Ares and Athena found glory in the wars that the mortals on Earth were fighting. They took sides against each other. Ares enjoyed the violence and bloodshed and Athena thought of ways to use strategy for glory and victory, but, in the end, they both loved war in different ways. When the Greeks believed in this god and goddess it led to centuries of senseless fighting.

THE BATTLE OF TROY

A major battle that took place where Ares and Athena were on opposite sides was the Trojan War. The Greeks ultimately won this war, which means that Athena had the final victory. Although Ares and Athena were imaginary, the Trojan War did take place although it was written more as a legend than historical fact.

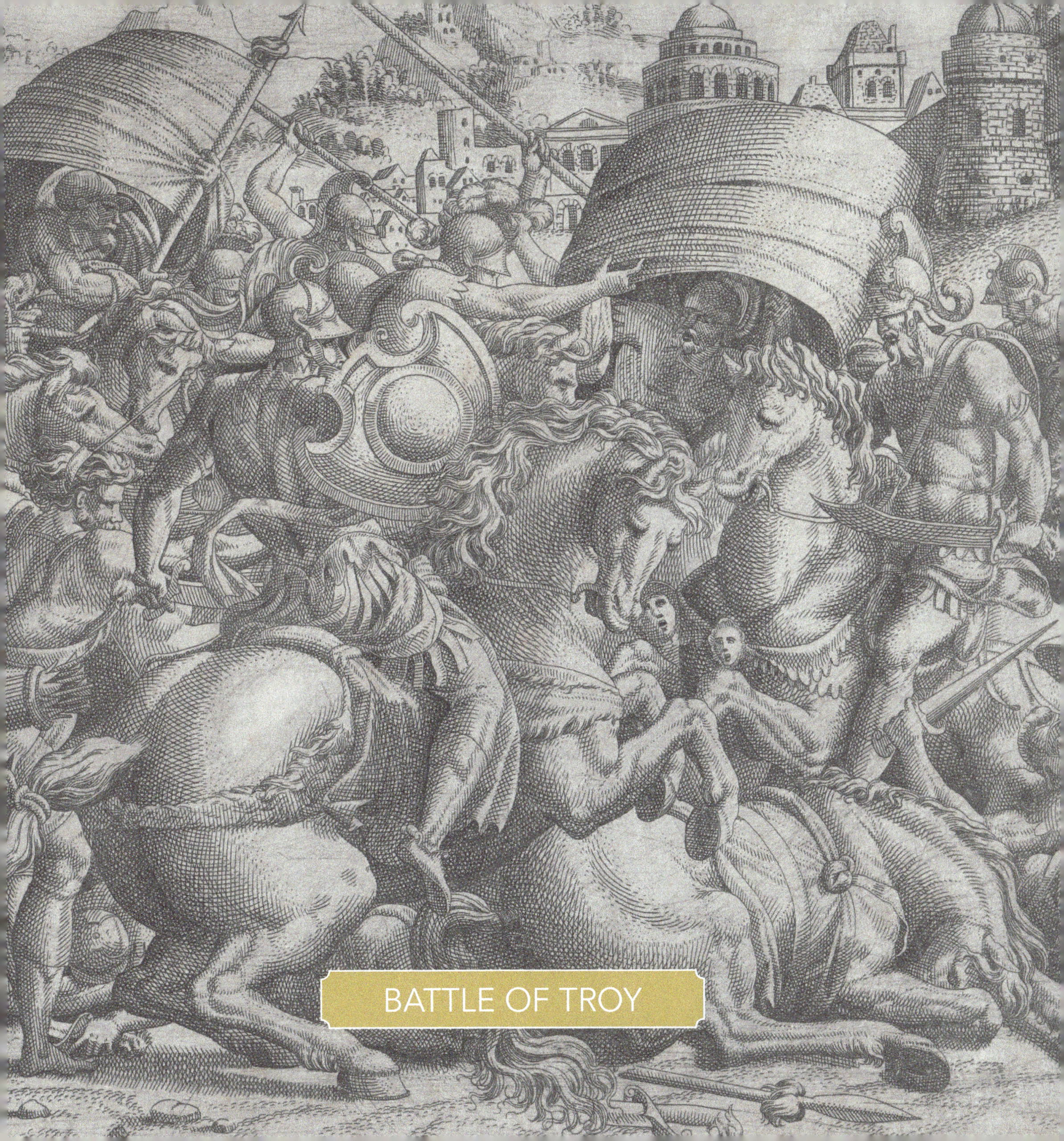
BATTLE OF TROY

It is one of the most famous tales in all of Greek mythology and today historians believe that some of the details might be correct and true, while other details may have been fiction created by the authors who wrote about it.

HOW THE TROJAN WAR WAS STARTED

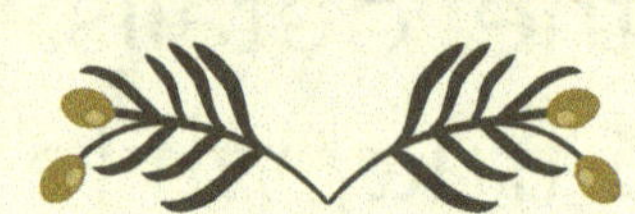

The gods and goddesses were celebrating on Mount Olympus. A goddess named Eris who liked to stir up trouble was upset because she was not invited. She wrote "to the most beautiful" on an apple made of gold and threw it into the party in front of three of the most beautiful goddesses. Those goddesses were Aphrodite, the goddess of love, Athena, the goddess of war, and Hera, Zeus's wife.

HERA, ATHENA AND ERIS IN THE TROJAN WAR

They began to fight with each other and asked Zeus to settle the argument, but he suggested that they let a mortal by the name of Paris say who the most beautiful goddess was.

THE JUDGMENT OF PARIS

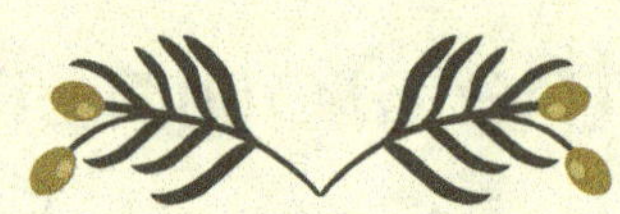

None of the goddesses were as confident as they should have been, so they each offered Paris a bribe and the bribes were all tempting. However, Paris liked the bribe that Aphrodite offered the best. She offered him the most beautiful woman in the world. Her name was Helen. Paris wanted Helen for his own, so he picked Aphrodite as the most beautiful. Athena and Hera were furious.

PARIS

HELEN

THE MOST BEAUTIFUL WOMAN IN THE WORLD

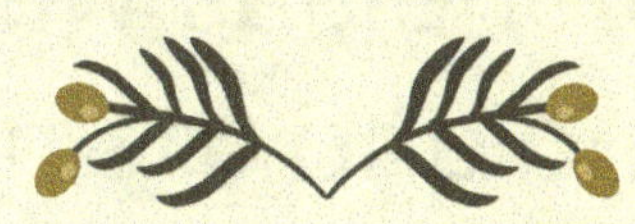

There was a problem though because Helen was going to be married soon. Many men in Greece wanted to marry Helen because she was so beautiful. Her father, the Spartan king, asked them to give an oath that they would protect whomever he chose for Helen's husband.

A man named Menelaus was selected to be Helen's husband and the new Spartan king. Aphrodite brought Paris to Sparta so he could be a guest at the wedding feast, even though Paris was a Trojan and the Trojans were enemies of the Spartans. When Menelaus had to leave on business, Paris charmed Helen and took her with him back to the city of Troy.

STATUE OF ABDUCTION OF HELEN

THE TROY ANCIENT CITY

When Menelaus returned and realized his wife had been kidnapped, he was furious. He called together the warriors who had promised their help when they made an oath. A fleet of one thousand warships was assembled and the warriors traveled over the water to the city of Troy.

THE GODS TOOK SIDES

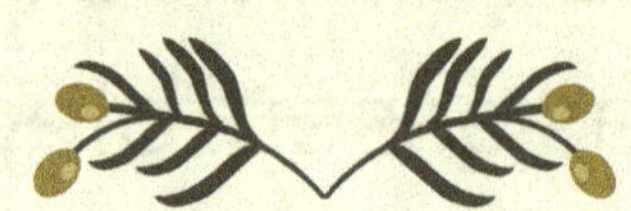

The war between the Greeks and the Trojans went on for nine years. Finally, the gods and goddesses were getting tired so they got involved. This is the place in the story where Athena and Ares were pitted against each other. Both Athena and Hera were still angry with Paris for not saying they were the most beautiful so they sided with the Greeks.

HERA

Poseidon, the god of the sea, sided with the Greeks as well. Aphrodite, Artemis, and Apollo all sided with the Trojans. With the gods and goddesses involved the battle became more violent than ever.

PARIS AND MENELAUS

At one point, to stem the bloodshed, it was decided that Menelaus and Paris should fight hand to hand for Helen and that the winner would have her for his wife. Paris was no match for Menelaus and he was about to die until Aphrodite helped him and he fled back to Troy. This could have been the end of the battle, but the Greeks were insulted by the cowardice of their enemies so they wanted to continue the battle. The goddess Athena and the goddess Hera wanted them back in the fight as well.

BATTLE BETWEEN MENELAUS AND PARIS

DIOMEDES

GODS ON THE BATTLEFIELD

The battle continued to wage on. The goddess Hera and the goddess Athena joined forces with a great mortal warrior by the name of Diomedes to fight against Athena's half brother, Ares, the god of war. The goddesses helped Diomedes to place his spear right in the middle of Ares's chest.

The god of war yelled out in pain so loudly that all the warriors in the battle heard him. His pride was wounded too, because a mortal had injured him, so he retreated to Mount Olympus to heal his wound.

When Ares came back to the battle, Athena managed to make him fall to the ground again.

MOUNT OLYMPUS

THE TROJAN HORSE

The war between the two enemies, the Greeks and Trojans, went on for 10 years. However, it was war strategy that eventually meant a victory for them. Paris and many others had died in battle, but Helen had not been returned to Greece. The Greeks built an enormous wooden horse and the Greek soldiers hid inside.

When the Trojans came out to the battlefield all they saw was the horse and one solitary Greek soldier. He explained to them that the Greek army had been defeated and gone home. He also relayed the message that the horse had been built in honor of the goddess Athena. The Greeks hoped that the Trojans would destroy the horse so the goddess would take her wrath upon them.

The Trojans pulled the beautiful wooden horse through the gates and into the center of the city. Inside the horse, the Greek soldiers kept completely quiet until nightfall. Then they unlatched the gates to the city to let the rest of the Greek army inside. They burned down the city. Helen was returned to her husband and the battle of Troy was over. The Greek army and Athena had finally won.

SUMMARY

War is filled with violence, but ultimately war strategy won the Trojan War as it has won many others. The intelligence of Athena won out over her bloodthirsty half-brother Ares.

Awesome! Now that you've read about Ares and Athena, you may want to read more information about Greek goddesses in the Baby Professor book *The Female Goddesses of the Olympian – Ancient Greece – Mythology.*

BABY PROFESSOR
EDUCATION KIDS